Tressanela Noosepickle
where are you now?

Unique perspectives of some most unusual,
astonishing, and hilarious authentic names

BRUCE RUTHERFORD

TRAFFORD

• Canada • UK • Ireland • USA •

Note for Librarians: A cataloguing record for this book is available from Library and
Archives Canada at www.collectionscanada.ca/amicus/index-e.html
ISBN 1-4120-9186-1

Printed on paper with minimum 30% recycled fibre.
Trafford's print shop runs on "green energy" from solar, wind and other
environmentally-friendly power sources.

Offices in Canada, USA, Ireland and UK

Book sales for North America and international:
Trafford Publishing, 6E–2333 Government St.,
Victoria, BC V8T 4P4 CANADA
phone 250 383 6864 (toll-free 1 888 232 4444)
fax 250 383 6804; email to orders@trafford.com
Book sales in Europe:
Trafford Publishing (UK) Limited, 9 Park End Street, 2nd Floor
Oxford, UK OX1 1HH UNITED KINGDOM
phone +44 (0)1865 722 113 (local rate 0845 230 9601)
facsimile +44 (0)1865 722 868; info.uk@trafford.com
Order online at:
trafford.com/06-0940

10 9 8 7 6 5

Who hath not owned,
with rapture-smitten frame,
the power of grace,
the magic of a name.

Thomas Campbell
1777-1844

To Jill, Dean, Sarah, and Bob
who, without a name,
would probably be known as "hey you."

Special thanks to Doug Hanson
whose contributions added to the
quality of this project.

Contents

Introduction

People's names fascinate me. I'm not sure why. It's one of those mysterious fixations many of us have, and can't shake loose. It probably has to do with the fact that everyone must have a name, and it's assigned to us at a time when we have the least say in the matter. Then the darned thing, good or bad, identifies us for a lifetime, unless we change it. A woman who marries, of course, customarily changes her surname to that of her husband.

I suppose you could call me an "onomatomaniac." This is a humorous word unofficially coined some years ago, which is defined as "one who has a mental condition characterized by an obsession of names."

Names never meant a thing to me until sometime in the early 1980s when I saw a rather bizarre authentic name in a newspaper or magazine, and jotted it down. A hobby or mania of sorts had begun.

Anything and anyone became a source for a "find"; telephone books, yearbooks, obituaries ... anything that might contain a person's name. It's a kick to have someone who knows I'm a name nut come up to me and say, "I have a name for you." Or sometimes in a social situation when I let my onomatomania be known I get a response like, "I went to high school with a guy named Jack Frost."

My efforts on the pages to follow consists of some unique perspectives of the best of the bunch collected over a period of years.

If you're the owner, or I should say renter, of an unusual name, it's possible that it might appear in this book. Just on that remote chance, please accept it in the spirit for which it's intended; to have some fun, not to defame or ridicule.

I hope you enjoy reading my book as much as I enjoyed writing it.

Bruce Rutherford
Downers Grove Illinois
March, 2006

A good name is rather to be
chosen than great riches.

Proverbs 22:1

A Glimpse at the Origin of Names

Many books have been written about the origin and evolution of names. The study of names, which is called onomastics (from onoma, the Greek word for name), is quite interesting.

Adam and Eve were suitably named. Their names are of Hebrew origin; Adam meaning "man of earth," and Eve meaning "life." In early history, names were derived from abstract qualities, deity, or personal characteristics.

This biblical couple had no surname. Who needed a second name with only two persons in the world? Whether or not the Garden of Eden story is allegorical is debatable, but there were so few people many centuries ago, and most of them didn't travel far from their birthplace, that there was no need for more than one name.

As the population of the world increased, and small villages became more urbanized, and the fact that many people had the same name, distinctions had to be made. Certain names were so popular that a village could easily have had more than half of its people using the same name. A second name became a necessity.

According to the Social Security Administration the four most common surnames in the United States are Johnson, Smith, Brown, and Jones. There's good reason for the frequency of these names. When a man chose to adopt a second identifying name one of the following sources was customarily used:

Father's first name – e.g. Johnson, which came from "John's son" or Williams, which came from "of William." Jones has its origin in "of John."

Occupation – e.g. Smith, Miller, Tanner, Weaver, Sawyer, Baker, Farmer.

Personal characteristic – e.g. Brown , White, Little, Long, Swift, Strong.

Geographic area – e.g. Woods, Lake, Hill, Rivers, Fields, Meadows, Valley.

Because it was a male dominated world when surnames appeared, and the fact that America was settled for the most part by people from England, there's little wonder that Johnson, Smith, Brown, and Jones are so common as family names.

As time progressed, many of these second name selections became overused, and people had to strive for more distinction. Practically anything was given consideration; items of property, animals, food, and drink were often chosen.

Surnames appeared such as Lumber, Bucket, Ox, Pump, Buzzard, Cabbagestalk and even Outhouse. Many of these names have become obsolete over the years, no doubt due mostly to the subsequent owners tiring of being the object of jokes and ridicule, but some of them still exist today.

The Social Security Administration reports that there are almost two-million different surnames in the United States. When you consider the infinite amount of first names that can be assigned to each of this vast number of family names, quite a few entertaining and astonishing personal monikers have come into existence.

So, let's have a look …

I don't care what the newspapers say about me,
so long as they spell my name right!

Timothy "Big Tim" Sullivan
1862-1913

The Last Shall Be First

You've probably noticed that the first few pages of your telephone directory consist mostly of business names with an "A" as the first letter. Often the name starts with a double or triple "A" in order to assure the business of having its name appear at the beginning of the directory.

Compose a name for your enterprise that's easy to find in the phone book, and calls from potential customers should be brisk, no doubt is the philosophy behind that.

The desire for a certain position in the telephone book isn't always for commercial benefit, though. For some people, being listed <u>last</u> in the directory provides prestige and satisfaction.

If you have this particular need, and your last name

starts with a "Z" followed by a couple of letters near the end of the alphabet, such as in Zyvec, chances are you'll get your wish. If you're lucky enough to have your last name begin with "ZZ", you're just about assured of having the distinction of being the last listing; and hooray for you.

But, still, this is no guarantee that your fellow citizens will see your name in that final entry. Some people have added many Z's to the beginning of their surname, some by legal authorization, some without, just to achieve that coveted last position.

For example …

A fellow named **Zachary Zzra** had established the last entry in the telephone directory of his city of residence. Much to his chagrin, in the next issue, he was replaced by one Vladimir Zzzzzzzbakov. Legal name or not, Vladimir began to enjoy the elation of seeing his name as the last listing.

Not be outdone, Zachary had seven Z's added to his last name, and now sporting the name Zachary Zzzzzzzzzra reclaimed that desired final spot in the next issue of his city's telephone book. Mysteriously, Vladimir's name never appeared again.

Then there's the case of Neil McDonagh …

Neil didn't like the fact that his name was mingled with all the names beginning with "Mc" in the telephone directory of his residential city.

He got the brainstorm of having his name listed last, and thereby gaining that special recognition he so needed. He actually went to court and had his name legally changed to **Zebedee Zzpp**.

Neil, or I should say Zebedee, achieved that last entry, and is enjoying life with his energetically-sought status.

While searching through the telephone books of various cities in the United States at the local library I found some more names for which the owners, I imagine, made a special effort to get nestled in that prestigious last listing.

Although I doubt if the surnames of these fine fellows appear on their birth certificates the same as we're about to see, they're authentic positions in tele-phone directories.

I'd like you to meet ...

Zebo Zzzent
Zelmo Zzzzip
Gene Zzzzycan
Zyzzy Zzrysxxy
Vladimir Zzzzyd
and
Archimedes Zzzyandottie

Gentlemen, you're first in my book!

What's in a name?
That which we call a rose
by any other name
would smell as sweet.

William Shakespeare
1564-1616

3

Birth Event Zealotry

What to name the baby; a common problem for many parents expecting a newcomer to the family.

Many books and booklets have been written about selecting a name for a newly-born. All of the authors caution their reader to resist the temptation to be humorous or cute when giving a name to the family addition.

Psychologists who have researched this subject tell us that an unusual or humorous name can possibly break the psyche of a child, and affect his or her personality, popularity, and future success in professional life. It's also been determined that students with more common names are given better grades than those with unusual or unpopular names.

There's no doubt that giving a child a name is an

important and delicate matter. Some parents, though, haven't resisted the temptation to be humorous or cute when giving a first name, and sometimes middle name, to their baby. Some wild and wacky names have been foisted on children.

To some parents the birth of a child can be such a joyous event that those with a suitable family name have concocted a name for their baby to reflect their jubilation or the newcomer's cherished existence, as if the little one would never grow out of babyhood.

For instance, there's Mr. and Mrs. Darling …

A son was born to them some years ago, which was a most welcome occasion. So welcome that he chooses to go through life using the initials of his first and middle name.

He's known as "W.B."

Can't blame him. He was saddled with …

Welcome Baby Darling

Then there's Mr. and Mrs. Dove.

When a lovable little girl entered their lives, temptation got the better of them in the naming process.

They came up with …

Lil Lovey Dove

A Mr. and Mrs. Joy were presented with a bundle of joy from Heaven.

Their family name also influenced them to get cute with their baby girl's lifetime appellation.

So, unless she marries, she'll always be …

Comfort Joy

When the stork visited Mr. and Mrs. Gluck with a daughter, they gave her the name of Heidi.

No problem there, but they couldn't resist showing what a delicacy they had when assigning her a middle name.

Heidi's full name is …

Heidi Yum-Yum Gluck

A Mr. and Mrs. Kidd have a family name that could lend itself to temptation if a newcomer joined the household.

Parenthood did indeed enter their lives when a son was born to them. Evidently, when matching-up his given name with the family name they neglected to consider that their little guy would grow into adulthood.

Mr. and Mrs. Kidd presented us with …

Winsome Kidd

Then we have Mr. and Mrs. Daub.

It seems like their last name couldn't be conducive to pinning something goofy on a newcomer to the family. After twelve years of marriage a son was finally born to them.

This was an event that was long desired, so they gave the little tyke the distinguished name ...

Zipadeedoo Daub

If the family name is Person, and the Mrs. is expecting, and each parent-to-be has the bent to be excessively elated about the birth event, something wacky just might be foisted on the newcomer in the naming function.

A certain Mr. and Mrs. Person did indeed succumb to the temptation.

The birth was a healthy baby girl, and on her birth certificate appears ...

Precious Person

This one is something else.

A husband and wife with the unusual surname of Today were certainly jubilant about the birth of their new little one.

Before they came back down to earth, the innocent bundle of humanity was named ...

Oh Heavenly Glory I'm Born Today

If the stork is scheduled to make a call, and the family name is Blessing, the little package of joy might be in for one heckuva name to have to live with.

It happened in this Blessing household.

A little girl was delivered and her birth certificate shows ...

Fairy Blessing

If your last name is Small, and your newcomer is a delight, as most of them are, you might be compelled to do what this Mr. and Mrs. Small did.

They dubbed their little gal ...

Delight Small

Then there a Mr. and Mrs. Gibbs.

It could be that they noticed a twinkle in the eye of their little new arrival of the female persuasion. Or it could be that her birth gave them a twinkle.

She was named ...

Twinkle Gibbs

And last, but certainly not least, a Mr. and Mrs. Collins had a way of telling the world that this birth event was their final go at it.

The innocent little newcomer was pinned with ...

The Last Collins

Some new parents, family name permitting, sure can get excessively taken-in by the swirl of a birth and the naming process, can't they?

But we're just getting warmed-up here. Let's have a look at some more parental shenanigans of a different sort.

Sticks and stones may break my bones,
but names will never hurt me.

Margaret Miller
1915-1994

4

A Christian Name if You Please

According to Webster, the informal definition of the word Christian is "human, civilized, decent."

I learned an interesting fact while gathering the background for this book. In the country of France, as stated by civil law, a newborn is allowed to bear only a Christian first name, or a name to honor an historical figure. City hall officials in that country will refuse to record in the birth registry any name that doesn't appear to conform to the law.

I imagine the philosophy of the French lawmakers, in addition to maintaining a sense of decorum in their country, was to save a child from a ridicule and possible damage to his or her psyche, making life more difficult than it should be.

Although we name collectors who keep an eye

peeled for the bizarre name would have to look for a different hobby, perhaps the United States should've considered the French way of name acceptance earlier in our history.

But, until our country makes amends, as we saw in the previous chapter, some parents with a feasible surname will foist some clever and wacky name combinations on their innocent newcomer. The result can often make life uncomfortable for the additional family member, but sometimes the bearer of the name carries it with pride, and enjoys the attention it brings.

A case in point would be the son of a Mr. and Mrs. Pickle. (one heckuva family name to begin with, don't you think?)

Some years ago they brought a little boy into the world, and decided to amuse themselves by assigning him the first name of Dill.

So, **Dill Pickle** began his life.

Dill, now a retired carpenter, says, "my name has given me a lot of trouble in my lifetime. I've had hotel reservations canceled, dinner reservations refused, and even credit cards closed before I got a chance to use them. It's been almost impossible for me to cash checks away from home, and there's no way I can make a collect call; the operators always think I'm joking, and hang-up on me."

But, all in all, Dill says that he has come to enjoy his name, and living with the attention it brings. He once won some money in an odd name contest, being judged to have the oddest name of all the entrants.

There's quite a number of names out there like Mr. Pickle's. It's amazing how some parents decide to get cute with their baby's name just because their family name allows this temptation. I certainly wouldn't call them Christian names, but they're entertaining, and make the life of an onomatomaniac a blast.

The names to follow are just a few of the many zany monikers of its type that exist in our culture.

Let's start with the female side of the ledger. Some parents had birds on the brain when naming their new little girl.

If the family name is suggestive of a bird, as in Robbins, the temptation to be clever with baby's given name just might get the better of you, as it did for this mom and dad.

I'd like you to meet …

Nesta Robbins

How about a Mr. and Mrs. Droppings.

How much careful thought did they give when naming their precious little girl? The compulsion to be clever sure dimmed their outlook. This is something else.

Say hello to …

Robbin Droppings

At least they added an extra "b" to give her some dignity.

·⌒·

Then there's Mr. and Mrs. Buzzard.

With their family name the bird concept really captured their fancy. All three names got in the theme.

Meet …

Robin Bird Buzzard

I wonder if they add to the fun by claiming the stork brought little Robin.

·⌒·

Let's get another one of God's creatures in here.

If your family name is Rabbit, and a baby girl is born to the household, the lure to get cute with her name could obscure any consideration for her future.

It did in one hare-brained case.

I'd like you to meet …

Bunny Rabbit

You have to wonder if Bunny particularly likes salads.

·⌒·

It could be that the owners of the next two appellations were born in the month of December.

With that as a possibility, conducive family names, and the inclination of the parents to be clever, we have a great formula for interesting names with which a couple of our fair ladies have to live.

May I present …

Holly Wreath

and

Christmas Carroll

I hope the holiday season is their favorite time of the year.

⁓

Moving over to the men's side.

The common name Harry can sometimes stir the imagination of parents, depending on the family name.

A Mr. and Mrs. Beard gave in to temptation when selecting a name for their new little guy.

Meet …

Harry Beard

Harry no doubt is an adult by now. I wonder if he does wear a beard.

⁓

Then there's Mr. and Mrs. Scull.

Although their last name isn't spelled with a "k", they still thought they'd get creative with their new little guy's name.

Or maybe it's not Mom and Dad's cleverness at all; perhaps they just like the name Harry.

I'd like you to meet …

Harry Scull

The name has sort of a morbid sound, doesn't it?

I have a couple more interesting Harry names, but they're in Chapter 16 for a certain reason.

The surname Eve is one of the two-million or so that exist in the United States, although quite rare. Even so, sooner or later some Mr. and Mrs. Eve had to express their creativity after a son was born to them.

Whether or not this is a Christian name is debatable, but it sure is Christian sounding.

May I introduce …

Adam Eve

I wonder if there's an Eve Adam out there. If you read this, Eve, contact me.

You certainly don't hear the family name Tank very often. In fact, I never heard of it until I came across the name I'm about to share with you.

Eventually, a Mr. and Mrs. Tank who were blessed with a son had to come-up with this appellation.

Meet …

Sherman Tank

I wonder if Sherm ever served in the military. If so, it just had to be in the Tank Corps.

Here are six more names in which the family name was ready, willing, and able to receive a given name to create a familiar combination.

May I present ...

Olive Pitt
Rock Pile
June Bride
Snow White
Amber Lights
and
April Showers

In these names the parents made a cute short statement with baby's name because the family name opened the temptation.

I'd like you to meet ...

Inita Mann
Justa Duck
Cora Apple
Justin Case
Doris Closed
and
Isabelle Ringing

In some cases the middle name is necessary to make the complete statement.

Say hello to ...

Janet Isadore Bell

and

Margaret Wears Black

The two ladies in the preceding case can hide their parents' fun by abbreviating or omitting their middle names, but this gal wasn't so lucky. She's stuck, with or without her middle name.

We welcome ...

Ima June Bugg

Sometimes the ordinary name Ann used for a middle name fits right into mom and dad's penchant to be clever, as it did for Mr. & Mrs. Hardy and Mr. & Mrs. Clyde after a daughter joined the family.

Meet ...

Laurel Ann Hardy

and

Bonnie Ann Clyde

The name May used as a middle name has stirred the imagination of some parents when assembling a name for their new baby girl, family name permitting.

Introducing …

Hazel May Call
June May March
Dorothy May Grow

Let's make May the first name, as did a mom and dad with the unusual family name of July.

They named their little girl …

May June July

The imagination of parents can be reflected in the middle initial of the baby's full name.

As in …

Dan D. Lyon
Park A. Carr
and
Watts D. Matter

I wonder if there's a Steve A Dore out there.

And sometimes cleverness is exhibited in the first and middle name initials, surname allowing.

Such as …

U. R. Smart
I. M. Strange

and how about these two …

I. M. Gay
I. M. Horny

Some parents huh?

In certain households parents don't just confine their naming eccentricities to one child.

For instance, there's a Mr. and Mrs. Leer. They brought a son and daughter into the world.

Their assigned monikers …

Gay Cava Leer

and

Crystal Shanda Leer

In this catch I don't know if Mr. and Mrs. Trout are fishing enthusiasts, but their family name sure is a lure to be clever with children's names.

They had two daughters, and they're hooked with

Brook Trout

and

Rainbow Trout

Then we have Mr. and Mrs. Ware.

They also graced society with two children. Their family name also stirred the creative juices.

I don't know the gender distribution in this find, but I'd like you to meet …

Silver Ware

and

Corning Ware

And finally, there's Mr. and Mrs. MacAllit.

A son was born to them. What possible zany appellation could they foist on him with a family name like that?

Say hello to ...

Watcha MacAllit

If our country had the Christian-name-only philosophy similar to France, would any of the preceding names have been approved by the birth registry?

Probably not ...... and I'd be collecting something other than names.

Giving a name, indeed is a poetic art,
all poetry, if we go to that with it,
is but a giving of names.

Thomas Carlyle
1795-1881

5

Members Only

Did you know that by virtue of your name alone you might qualify for exclusive membership to a club?

Some time after I involved myself in keeping a lookout for the off-beat name I discovered that owners (I prefer renters) of certain names, or a type of name, have organized themselves into clubs. I'm aware of seven such organizations, but I have a hunch there are more.

Certain given names or surnames, or the combination of the two, are so important to some of their holders that they either organize or join clubs to which they qualify.

My first name Bruce is relatively rare, and I've sometimes wondered if there's a Bruce Club out there. I tried a Google search, but came up empty. Heck, I'd join a Bruce Club if it existed, but I'm not so desirous as to initiate such an organization.

Let's start off with a club based on a last name.

The Fink Club

All persons with the surname Fink qualify for membership to this organization.

The club was originated for the purpose of giving members opportunity to console each other for the abuses of their name. For example, "you finked on me!" or "you're a rat fink!"

June 26th of each year is "National Fink Day." Anybody with the surname Fink is invited to attend a gala, which is held in Fink, Texas.

I wonder how many members fink out.

Then there's a club based on a customarily lady's first name.

The Betty Club

To qualify for membership to this organization you must be "Bettyborn." Anyone who has the given name Betty on her birth certificate is welcome to join this exclusive society of women; any other spelling is ineligible.

The club was founded by a Betty Wilder and Betty Patterson who, on a whim, wondered how many Bettys there are in America. Of course, not every Betty in

America has heard of The Betty Club, or would join if she did.

The cartoon character Betty Boop has been adopted as the club's logo, and her facsimile appears on the stationery, buttons, T-shirts, and other items.

If she were still alive, Bette Davis, wouldn't be allowed to join. She was born Ruth Elizabeth Davis, anyway.

⁓

The Lois Club

Similar to The Betty Club, this organization is open to membership for all women named Lois.

The purpose for the founding of this exclusive club is that the given name Lois is disappearing from usage. The members want to preserve their beloved moniker.

The Lois Club is nationwide with many chapters, and hopes to go international.

I know a lady whose middle name is Lois. I wonder if she'd be allowed to join. It seems like she should based on the club's reason for being.

⁓

The Jim Smith Society

To qualify for membership to this organization your surname must be Smith with a given name of either James, Jim, Jimmie, Jimmy or Jamie.

The society has a wide membership, including

women, because of the first name flexibility. Its purpose is to give pride to people with this rather bland name.

According to the club's president, Jim Smith (who else?), "when your name is Jim Smith you tend to feel pretty ordinary. Our goal is to make all Jim Smiths stick out their chests, and stand tall." I imagine that includes the lady members too.

The strict spelling eligibility of the last name makes me wonder about those Jims with the last name spelled Smithe, but pronounced the same as Smith. Don't they deserve this morale support too?

The Fred Society

Similarly, this organization was founded to give pride and a sense of belonging to people with the first name Fred, or a name that's usually shortened to Fred. After all, Fred is such an unexciting first name.

As does the other clubs, this society is nationwide, and has an annual convention.

I imagine that there's a female name or two that's shortened to Fred by her friends. So I wonder if there are any women members, as there are in the Jim Smith Society.

Mikes of America

The only qualification for membership to this

organization is that your given name be Michael or Mike. Its purpose is to put a person named Michael in the White House. No president has ever had this first name. They came close in the 1988 national election when Michael Dukakis was the Democrat Party nominee.

Again, I wonder if this club allows female members. I personally know a lady whose given name is Michael.

I've saved the best for last.

The My Name is a Poem Club

To qualify for membership in this club your given name and last name must rhyme. Also, your last name must be that of your parents; rhyming by way of marriage is ineligible.

Hugh Blue was the founder and the first president of this name-rhyming society.

I don't have a membership roster, but I've come across many names that I'm sure would qualify.

Here are just a few …

Jill Hill
Max Sax
Dale Frail
Frank Plank
Floyd Boyd
Alice Palace

Mollie Wollie
Lester Hester

How about a triple-rhymer. They'd love this guy.

Barry Derryberry

These two fellows should qualify.

Paysoff Tinkoff
Thirupathy Sabapathy

What if your name looks like a poem, but doesn't rhyme?

Such as …

Sean Bean

My guess is his application would be denied.

Finally, I think the ineligibility of the rhyming after marriage rule should be reconsidered. With names like these four ladies agreed to live with after getting hitched, they should at least get honorable mention.

Maybe you'll agree.

Ann Stann
Julia Gulia
Alma Palma
Willowdean Dean.

Ladies, don't tolerate this ostracism, start your own club!

If you know of any other organizations based on people's names, please let me know.

Three things I never lends –
my 'oss, my wife and my name.

Robert Smith Surtees
1803-1864

6

He Lives Down the Road a Piece

Have you ever walked or driven along a rural road and noticed the names on the mail boxes?

Many of them have a certain rustic flavor. It seems that a significant number of people who were raised and live in rural communities have names that are characteristically non-urbane.

Many years ago when the television production *The Andy Griffith Show* was conceived, some of the characters were given names like Gomer Pyle, Barney Fife, Ernest T. Bass, and the like. No doubt the intent was to lend a typical small town sound to these names. Legendary comedian of a few decades ago, Jonathan Winters, among his many impersonations, had a bumpkin-like character whom he called Elwood Suggins. The flavor of the name and rural-town America go together.

With my always eagle-eye open for names of various types, I've discovered some that certainly are suitable for this theme. I don't know if the persons with the names to follow grew up in the hinterlands, but their ascribed appellations sure have a distinct rural quality.

I imagine all of these names would be considerations for characters in a television show with a rural setting by scriptwriters. Maybe you'll agree.

Let's start off with …

Arlus Blunk

Great name for a rural mail box, don't you think?

Then we have …

Elvin Dumps

Sounds like a small-town fellow to me.

On the ladies side how about …

Mattie Crump

Marvelous name for a spinster in a rural setting.

Here's a lady with a raht purty name …

Maybelle Snorf

I love that one for some reason.

Then there's …

Emmitt Suggs

He just has to be from the hinterlands.

. ᴗ .

Our next fellow with a rural-flavored name certainly should be a pig farmer …

Nunley Lard

At least he should be a portly gent.

. ᴗ .

Here's a terrific name for a neighbor who lives down the road a piece …

Norwood Whooper

. ᴗ .

Now this lady surely must have grown-up in rural-town America …

Quetta Lumpkin

. ᴗ .

Here's a great name for the wife of a pig farmer, or maybe just a lady who raises pigs …

Daisy Piggies

Remember, these are real names, folks.

. ᴗ .

A few more names whose owners just might've been born and raised in rural America.

Say howdy to …

Elsie Blickle
Luther Petty

Duncan Funk
Orban Skaggs
Elmer Snoddy
Eldon Wooters
and my favorite tiller of the fields ...
Silas Turnipseed

Lots of fun.

Let's have a look at how marriage can sometimes affect a lady's name.

Sweet, as the sweetest melodies
filling my soul with ecstasy,
sweeter than all things to me,
the sound of my sweetheart's name.

Will D. Cobb
1876-1930

7

I Take Thee and Your Name Too

After the wedding it's traditional in our society for the bride to give up the surname to which she's been accustomed for so many years and assume the surname of the groom.

Most of our fair ladies who marry make this transition without significant consequence. But for some brides, the pairing of her given name with the last name of her new husband can result in an amazing and sometimes hilarious combination.

Of course, it has to be said that nowadays, due to professionalism and feminism, some new wives don't change their surname at all.

Women in show business who marry often retain their original last name for professional reasons. A cute story in this regard involves movie actress Kirstie

Alley. She was born with the surname Alley, and her first husband was a fellow named Robert Alley. Same name either way.

But situations like that are rare. Most brides experience a name change, some of which are sure something else.

Let's have a look.

Starting with four ladies whose given name is Rose.

First we have Rose Stein.

She entered holy matrimony with none other than Frank Bloom.

She then became …

Rose Bloom

Then there's Rose Malyurek.

She accepted the marriage proposal of one Henry Flowers.

The result …

Rose Flowers

Third up is Rose Leitz

Romance entered her life with Howard Bush. They soon became husband and wife.

Her new name …

Rose Bush

And last up is Rose Kipnis.

She chose to accept the marriage proposal of David Rose, knowing she'd be ...

Rose Rose

Staying with the Rose theme, I came across a great story of a gal with the maiden surname Rose.

Her parents thought it cute to give her the first name Wild. So during her growing-up years she was Wild Rose, which is a great name in itself for a name collector.

Little did Mr. and Mrs. Rose know who Wild would eventually marry. She settled down with Thomas Bull.

Thus, Wild Rose became ...

Wild Bull

Here's a rather botanical match-up.

Myrtle Sheber and George Lily were joined in holy matrimony.

Perhaps the bridal bouquet included some myrtle and lily. The bride is now ...

Myrtle Lily

Sometimes marriage can make the new name of a bride that of a well-known name in history.

For example, when Helen Novotny wedded a fellow named Henry Keller, she became ...

Helen Keller

Within the same theme we have a lady who grew-up as Eva Feurman.

After her wedding to Theodore Braun, she kept tradition, and assumed her husband's surname.

Society now knows her as ...

Eva Braun

And at rare times the name combination of a bride can result in a statement.

One of our fair ladies named Iona Johnson accepted the proposal of a fellow with the unusual name Lyle Hotel.

Her drivers license now shows ...

Iona Hotel

Wouldn't it be something else if she did own a hotel?

This one is some coincidence.

When a Mr. and Mrs. Eldred gave the ordinary name Mary to their new daughter, how could they know what her married surname would be?

Mary joined hands in holy matrimony with none other than Samuel Christmas.

Season's greetings to …
Mary Christmas

Some women hope to marry into money.

Penny Knowles did it in a most unusual way. She had the cents to marry Robert Nickel.

Following tradition, she became …
Penny Nickel

Here's a colorful couple.

All this lady had to do was change colors with her family name after she entered wifehood.

When Edith Brown was ready to settle down, who came into her life but Edward Green.

So, after the wedding …
Edith Brown became **Edith Green**

Hope they've always been in the black, never in the red, and have never felt blue.

Here's a truly good find.

A gal named Truly Gold (marvelous name for an unusual name book) must've been truly in love.

She agreed to marry a fellow named Cary Boring, knowing her name would become …
Truly Boring

On rare occasions all the bride has to do is change one letter of her last name after marriage.

For instance, Lucille Bleck accepted the call from cupid, and entered wedlock with Raymond Block.

She just had to replace one vowel with another.

Lucille Bleck became **Lucille Block**

This bride just had to replace a consonant.

Anna Boyce fell in love, and soon joined hands in marriage with a fellow named Martin Joyce.

Anna Boyce to **Anna Joyce**

And sometimes the bride doesn't have to change her name at all. This one is for Ripley's *Believe It or Not.*

Not only is the last name of each partner the same, but the first name of the bride when shortened to its common nickname is pronounced the same as the groom's

Christine Sanders accepted the marriage proposal of Kris Sanders. Thus …

Kris Sanders and **Chris Sanders** became husband and wife!

Here's a matrimonial name change that's reminiscent of an event in American history.

A lady named Pearl Hussey decided that Paul Harber was her life's partner; and he the same.

After the wedding she followed tradition and became ...

Pearl Harber

Harbor, as an inlet to anchor boats, is spelled with an "o", but this is still a great find for this chapter's theme.

⌒

Can an entertaining combination occur just by acquiring the title "Mrs." after a woman marries?

I communicated with the lady in this entry. She told me of the fun she has being a Mrs. in conjunction with her married surname.

In her single days she was Polly Palmer. She eventually married Rodney Sippy. The name Polly Sippy doesn't have a place in a book of unusual names, but how about ...

Mrs. Sippy

⌒

Not always does the bride take the surname of the groom. On rare occasions the groom takes the surname of the bride. Here's a great story.

A young woman with the name Tuesday Hood and a fellow named Robin Thursday entered holy matrimony.

Rather than Tuesday having to endure life as Tuesday Thursday (wouldn't that have been a doozy?), the couple decided to use the last name of the bride. They thought it would be the lesser of two evils for the groom to bear the burden.

The bride remains as Tuesday Hood, and the groom takes the slings and arrows of being **Robin Hood**.

Here's a lady I had the pleasure of meeting.

Although she's divorced now, she still uses her married name. She enjoys living with the name that marriage created for her.

As a single she was Tiffany Mayer. She eventually became the bride of Robert Glass.

And now she's ...

Tiffany Glass

Here's the closer. It's both astonishing and hilarious. And it's for real.

A gal named Lotta Rowe fell into eternal love with none other than Leonard Crapp. She accepted his proposal of marriage ... for better or for worse.

She faces society with her head held high as ...

Lotta Crapp

All great stuff.

In the next chapter there's more nuptial name fun of a different sort.

It would have saved trouble
had I remained Perkins from the first.
This changing of women's names
is a nuisance we are now happily outgrowing.

Charlotte Perkins Gilman
1860-1935

8

Till Death Do Us Part

Not all women who marry conform to the tradition of dropping their maiden name and taking their husband's surname.

At times the bride chooses to use both surnames separated by a hyphen, or she takes her husband's surname and substitutes her given middle name with her maiden surname. In England it's quite common for a bride to keep both family names hyphenated.

Amazing and funny surname coincidences can occur when certain couples enter marriage. It's a wonder how many entertaining name combinations happen to a guy and gal who fall in love and ultimately marry.

If the brides in the authentic name match-ups to follow had chosen to use both family surnames separated by a hyphen, or had substituted her middle name with her maiden last name, the result would be a hoot, and in some cases, a bit embarrassing.

Let's start with a lady who was known as Frieda Raggs in her single days.

She eventually married-up with a fellow named Kurt Riches.

Had she elected to use both surnames, she'd be …

Frieda Raggs-Riches

Then there's Ida Needle.

Being a love junkie for Harry Marks, she accepted his proposal of marriage.

Using both surnames, the name on her drivers license would appear as …

Ida Needle-Marks

Can you imagine the names on the wedding announcement of this coosome twosome:

A gal named Ruth Berndt joined hands in marriage with none other than William Wiener.

If Ruth insisted on hyphenating both family names, she'd be greeting society as …

Ruth Berndt-Wiener

Want that with pickles and mustard?

How about Allison Pickels (correct spelling) marrying up with Charles Mustard.

Dare she use both family names?

Allison Pickels-Mustard

Wash that frank down with a beer?

Elizabeth Beers had love brewing in her heart for Thomas Franks. She accepted his proposal of marriage.

If she used both surnames …

Elizabeth Beers-Franks

What brand of beer do you want?

The wedding announcement for this marital union had to have generated a few chuckles.

If the former Helen Miller had taken both family names after her wedding, she'd be a walking beer commercial. She married Herman Light.

So, she could be known as …

Helen Miller-Light

Here's another great name match-up that would make the bride a perpetual commercial.

Michelle Johnson and David Wax decided they couldn't live without each other, and became husband and wife.

Had Michelle opted for the dual surname …

Michelle Johnson-Wax

I wonder if the partners in this marriage are anglers.

Had Wendolyn Fisher decided to take the bait and use both family names after her wedding to Charles Fish, we'd know her as ...

Wendolyn Fisher-Fish

Here's a surname combo that creates an occupation.

Carolyn Gunn had a certain fellow with the rather ordinary name Larry Smith in her sights.

Carolyn Gunn-Smith?

The amazing coincidences continue.

One of our fair ladies name Bonnie Flint decided that a fellow named Timothy Stone was her eternal partner; and he the same. They were joined in connubial bliss.

If she hyphenated ...

Bonnie Flint-Stone

I wonder if there's a Barney-Rubble marriage out there.

There are winners and losers in the institution of

marriage. I have a couple of name match-ups that fall right into that theme.

First we have Mollie Superfine (interesting surname) who became the bride of Morris Winner.

Choosing to use both surnames the name on her check book would be ...

Mollie Superfine-Winner

And there's Mary Ellen Good.

After cupid's arrow brought eternal love into her life, she became the bride of Thomas Loser.

If she insisted on maintaining both last names ...

Mary Ellen Good-Loser

Loser might be said with a long "o", but it's great in print.

Hopefully this partnership was launched in church.

Bernice Christ and Warren Bless decided they couldn't live without each other, and entered holy matrimony.

It would be divine it she carried both names.

Bernice Christ-Bless

Christ might be pronounced with a short "i", but, again, it looks good in print.

This couple is just surrounded with love.

If you're the bride, and an incurable romantic, what better name could there be to have throughout life, particularly if you keep both surnames?

Lynette Lovely married David Love.

If I were her, I'd hyphenate.

Lynette Lovely-Love

If you like musicals, and you're familiar with *Annie Get Your Gun*, you'll like this one.

A lass named Carol Buttons married-up with a lad named Robert Bowes.

Carol, opting to keep both names, would be …

Carol Buttons-Bowes

Here's an interesting nuptial name nexus with a different twist.

A gal with the name Janice Mason during her single days, even after marriage, divorce, and remarriage couldn't escape a fun surname match-up.

First, Janice became wedded to Leonard Dixon. That, of course, created the dual-name, if she kept both names …

Janice Mason-Dixon

But the marriage failed.

Then, as life would have it, Janice fell in love with and married Howard Jarr.

Janice Mason-Jarr?

·〜·

This find could've been placed in the preceding chapter as a married surname requiring just the change of one vowel, but I saved it for here.

A gal named Sheila Olsen had the distinction of finding love with none other than a fellow named Paul Olson. They became husband and wife.

Sheila Olsen-Olson?

That wedding invitation had to have been a hoot.

·〜·

Five more to go.

One of our fair ladies with the name Sandra Clock took as her lawful wedded husband one Ralph Sharp.

Get me to the church on time!

If she insisted on keeping both family names ...

Sandra Clock-Sharp

Makes you wonder how punctual Sandra is.

·〜·

This find would really be something if the couple involved operated a flower shop.

Virginia Marigold joined hands in marriage with who else but Robert Plant.

Hyphenated ...

Virginia Marigold-Plant

·〜·

Despite the name coincidence, I hope the partners in this marriage are law-abiding citizens.

A lady with the unusual name Mimi Crooks saved her heart for a fellow named William Banks. And he discovered she had stolen his. They joined forces in marriage.

Dare she?

Mimi Crooks-Banks

Here's a hot one.

As fate would have it, Ginger Burner felt love cooking in her heart for none other than Martin Ovens. He the same.

They became husband and wife.

Does this name appear on her drivers license, etc.?

Ginger Burner-Ovens

And lastly.

Susan Dyer, surnames and all, accepted the marriage proposal of one Frank Rhea.

It had to be true love.

Susan Dyer-Rhea?

And so it goes.

Know anybody with a reversed name? Let's look at the next chapter.

I remember your name perfectly,
but I just can't think of your face.

William A Spooner
1844-1930

9

It's Penn Joe, not Joe Penn

During my high school years I had a classmate named Medford Howard. He wasn't in my particular den of friends, but we graduated the same year. I thought of him as the guy with the reversed name. That is, a name in which the last name is usually a first name, and vice versa.

A friend of mine told me that when she was in her teens she was employed by a man named Palmer Martin. Her mother was never sure of the correct order of the name. "Is it Palmer Martin or Martin Palmer?" she would occasionally ask.

Chances are, we all know, or have known a person with a reversed name. I can imagine the ever-present necessity of having to clarify the correct sequence of his name the owner of such an appellation has to deal with throughout life.

If you were a teacher viewing the roster of your students for the first time, and saw Mr. Howard's name, you'd probably wonder if the name is reversed in error, and have to get a clarification. Is it Howard Medford or Medford Howard?

I've come across some interesting reversed names along the way. Most of them are male because I can be sure they're given names.

I have a couple reversed names that I know belong to women, but I can't be certain if they're the result of parental creativity or marriage.

I'll share them with you.

Jordan Lucy

and

Anodea Judith

The reversed names I'm about to show you all belong to members of the male persuasion. It occurred to me while assembling this chapter that one of these fellows should start a reversed name club, if one doesn't already exist.

᷄

Let's start with this gent who no doubt is always primed for sequence clarification.

I'd like you to meet ...

Sparkman Scott

This chap's name probably has caused uncertainty ever since he started kindergarten.

Meet ...

Reynolds Dennis

For some reason I get a kick out of this one.

There can't be very many fellows with this first name out there.

May I introduce ...

Hathaway Harvey

Imagine the sequence clarifying this fellow has to deal with as he wends his way through life.

Say hello to ...

Hunt Henry

Here's a great reversed name find.

I don't envy this guy's constant need to confirm the correct order of his name.

Introducing ...

Woodrow Keith

Here are three more names with which the lessees, I imagine, have to live with the ongoing annoyance of sequence clarification.

Elkin Jack

Bates Burt
and
Austin Eddie

Some people with a reversed name have a double whammy. Not only is the correct order of their name confusing, but they probably have to clarify their gender affiliation as well. You can imagine this dialogue that a fellow named **Winfield Shirley** has to deal with on occasion:

In a gathering he might hear, "Shirley Winfield, is she here?" Or on a telephone call, "may I speak to a Miss or Mrs. Shirley Winfield?"

"You've got my name reversed, and I'm a he!" Winfield has to respond.

I wouldn't doubt that this chap has to endure that sort of exchange every so often.

I'd like you to meet …

Todd Amy

It would be interesting to learn what aggravating name sequence and gender clarifying situations this man has to confront.

May I introduce …

James Betty

And lastly, I'm sure this fine fellow knows what Winfield, Todd, and Jim have to deal with.

Say hello to ...

Willow Ruth

Like a Boy Scout, I'm sure the assignees of the appellations in this chapter are always prepared.

Gentlemen (and ladies), I hope you've maintained your sense of humor as you've had to clarify, clarify, clarify.

By the way, Penn Joe is an authentic name.

...yet leaving a name I trust
that will not perish in the dust.

Robert Southey
1774-1843

10

Named in Honor of ...

About two of every three babies born in this great nation of ours are given a name to honor another person, or the given name is influenced by the name of a relative, friend, or someone of notoriety, fictional or non-fictional.

The resurgence of the female name Jennifer in the 1970s, for example, most likely had its origin from the heroine in the popular movie *Love Story*. My daughter-in-law, born in that decade, is a Jennifer. I wouldn't be surprised if the current popularity of actress Jennifer Lopez has an influence on parents with a baby girl to name.

My daughter, Sarah, born in 1975 was named after a relative and the biblical Sarah. At the time a motion picture was influencing the name Jennifer, there was a biblical influence of the name Sarah. In her senior year at college Sarah shared a residential annex with six female students. Of the total seven, four were named Sarah!

In the men's realm, soon after Neil Armstrong stepped on the Moon, the name Neil suddenly became widely ascribed to male births.

My given name was influenced by the name of a friend of my parents. One of my two sons, Robert, was named after his maternal uncle and paternal grandfather. My other son's name, Dean, was influenced by the name of a professional athlete.

Quite possibly, your given name, and that of most of the people you know and love, was selected to honor someone, or was influenced by that of a known person.

The most common way of honoring another person with baby's name, of course, is when a father's first name and often middle name, is given to a son.

Sometimes this can be carried too far.

I came across a fascinating story that took place in the household of Mr. and Mrs. Eugene Jerome Dupuis. As nature would have it, they produced six sons.

The Dupuis's chose to honor Eugene (or possibly Eugene chose to honor himself, having a submissive wife) by giving all six of the boys as they entered the world the name **Eugene Jerome Dupuis Jr.**!

To prevent confusion in the household, the boys are identified by the number in order of their birth.

"Two and Four, it's your turn to do the dishes!"

⁓

A similar anecdote involves boxing great George Foreman.

He, along with Mrs. Foreman's help, fathered five sons and five daughters. Wow! I don't know the daughters' names, but dad sure was honored when the sons were named.

The lot of them were named George, and as in the Dupuis household, are known by the number of their birth.

⁓

Apparently, at times the baby will be named to honor the circumstances of the birth, as in the case of my paternal grandfather born way back in 1888.

He came into the world one frosty October morning on a farm in Boone County, Indiana. His parents honored the morning and location by naming him …

Frost Boone Rutherford

Grampa Frost passed away in 1963. He's missed by all.

⁓

How about this one.

A Mr. and Mrs. Joseph Florida, who resided in the state of Alabama, were blessed with a baby girl.

They put their ingenuity to work, and for her middle name honored the state of her birth.

What about the first name? May as well add another state.

Meet ...

Georgia Alabama Florida

Could baby's name be influenced by a product advertised on a billboard?

A future basketball legend, just born, lay nameless in his bassinet at the hospital. What to name this little guy.

His father glanced out the window and saw a billboard advertising the Elgin Watch.

And so, **Elgin Baylor** began his life.

At times, a president will be honored when the little newcomer is assigned a name.

When you have the surname of an infamous presidential assassin, give it some dignity by naming your newly born son after the victim.

I'd like you to meet ...

Abraham Lincoln Booth

Why not honor two presidents with baby's name?

In this instance, maybe one of the parents was a Democrat, and the other a Republican.

A certain Mr. and Mrs. Gibson brought a son into the world, and gave him the name …

Franklin Roosevelt Herbert Hoover Gibson

When Franklin has to occasionally sign his full name, is there ever enough room?

If your baby girl is born on Valentine's Day, you might be tempted to honor that special day with her name.

But what if the family name is already Valentine?

No problem, said Mr. and Mrs. Valentine who were in that very situation, let's go with …

Valentine Valentine

In this case I don't know if the parents of the little guy had the intent of honoring an historical person with the given name, or just wanted to be clever because the family name gave them the green lite.

I'll give them the benefit of the doubt for the theme of this chapter.

Introducing …

Henry Ford Carr

Speaking of cars, why not honor your personal passion for a certain type of automobile with the names of your children as they make their appearance in the world?

Mr. and Mrs. Donald Tonniges, sports car enthusiasts, produced four sons and a daughter from their assembly line.

Their names ...

Jaguar

Ferrari

Astin Martin

Austin Healy

and

Lancia Lemans

I wonder if the second name in the last three are middle names.

Would a baby be named to honor his father's business?

Way back in 1881 one Jesse Dubbs, who was in the oil refinery business, became the father of a son. The little guy, hopefully with the mother's permission, was named ...

Carbon Petroleum Dubbs

This zany name had no negative effect on Carbon's psyche. He followed in his father's footsteps in the refinery business, and invented what is known as the "Dubbs Process."

Carbon became a wealthy man.

As each baby arrives, why not honor the sound of the father's first name?

Not a bad idea, but what if the little ones just keep arriving and arriving and arriving?

A Mr. and Mrs. Ronny Craw had that concept in mind, but had to extend it to twelve births!

May I present …

Onny

Donny

Lonny

Vonny

Nonny

Yonny

Tonny

Shonny

Bonnie

Connie

Monnie

and

Johnnie

With this vast bunch I hope they have a lot of mon-ny.

Then there's Mr. and Mrs. Mickey Hickey (member of the poem club?)

They had the same idea in mind as the Craws, except in this case it honors the sound of each parent's name.

Mom is Vickey Hickey.

The Hickeys had just three children.

Their names ...

Dickey

Rickey

and

Nickey

Hope nobody in this family is ickey.

How would you like to be named after a mixed drink or a liquor?

A Mr. and Mrs. Lundeen also graced the world with three children.

Their assigned appellations ...

Chablis

Daquiri

and

Tequila

A toast to the Lundeen family! (maybe Dad's a bartender)

Possibly the most incredible case in which naming the little newcomer was influenced by the name of another person took place a little over a hundred years ago.

This one is something else.

A Mr. and Mrs. Bowman attended a circus in town, and were delighted by the antics of a clown who called himself "Oofty Goofty." Mrs. Bowman was in a family way at the time, and soon after, a son was born to the Bowmans.

These loving but apparent rustics gave him the name ...

Oofty Goofty Bowman

Oofty Goofty liked his name, and never tried to hide it.

And finally, the ultimate name with which to be honored.

A Mr. and Mrs. Christ, who happened to live in Bethlehem, Pennsylvania, received a bundle from Heaven.

It was a son.

I imagine the city of birth and the family name stirred the ingenuity of this mom and dad.

His name ...

Christ Christ

I'm sure having fun, aren't you?

More fun coming up.

A good name is better than a girdle of gold.

A French proverb

11

Appellative Determinism

Obviously I get a kick out of the various viewpoints that this name-collecting business creates. An especially fun area for me is discovering the name of a person that relates in some way to his or her occupation.

I imagine the name/occupation coincidence is something that all of us find particularly entertaining. There's a *Jerry Seinfeld* television show episode that includes a library tracer of overdue books with the last name "Bookman." The character *Kramer* says, "that's like being an ice cream vendor with the name cone."

There's a Latin proverb that goes "nomen est omen." I think that translates to "the name portends the future." Now, I don't know if that extends to a person's selection of profession, but I find it uncanny that many names relate to the livelihood of its owner. In some cases, you have to wonder if the family name did indeed give a subliminal nudge into the choice of career or occupation for some people.

I call this name/work relativity "appellative determinism."

Some names have a direct relationship to the profession, as in the case of an attorney with the surname Law. Others have a relationship of humorous irony, such as a dentist with the surname Panik.

I have a bunch of them.

Let's start off with some of my finds with a direct relationship.

Was the choice of profession by **Leroy Doctor** influenced by his family name? It sure makes you wonder.

He's a physician!

·⌒·

And what about **Ronald Footer**?

He chose podiatry for his life's work!

Hmmmm … interesting to say the least.

·⌒·

My appellative determinism theory points toward a positive verdict when you consider this case.

Courtney Justice decided law was the career for her.

She's an attorney!

⌇

Next we have **James Toothaker**.

Am I going to tell you he went into general dentistry?

Well, he won't fill a cavity, but he'll fix your smile.

He's an orthodontist!

Nomen est omen.

⌇

Meteorology is a science that deals with weather conditions.

So, **Kenneth Weathers** decided that was the profession for him.

He's a meteorologist!

Own up to it, Ken, didn't your name give you just a little nudge?

⌇

This theory of mine begins to pick-up some steam when you relate the names of these four practitioners to their career choice.

Dr. Martin Fish
Dr. Robert Lamb
Dr. Steven Beaver
Dr. Richard Sparrow

DVMs all ... Doctors of Veterinary Medicine!

⌇

Sometimes this name/profession correlation gets downright amazing.

How could a fellow named **Richard Bone** choose to be an osteopath, and that be nothing more than a mere coincidence?

Osteo is the Greek word for bone I hasten to add!

· ⌢ ·

Let's turn to religion.

Was there any influence by the family name for these two men, pray tell? They elected to enter the ministry.

A higher calling than just a name-nudge I suppose.

Rev. Edmund Gospel
Rev. Forester Church

· ⌢ ·

Here's an interesting biographical sketch.

A few decades ago, after completing high school, a young man enlisted in the military. After his hitch was up, rather than re-enlist, he elected to find work as a civilian.

He chose to learn the printing business.

Oh, his name? **Norman Printer**.

Hmmm …

· ⌢ ·

Now I'm really going to put this theory of mine over the top.

The career choice of **Richard Police**?
None other than law enforcement!

Next he's going to tell us he found the name of a psychiatrist with the surname Head.
I sure wish I could, but how about …
Lawrence Brain, Doctor of Psychiatry
Mental problem? See Dr. Brain.

There's a **Dr. Orth** who practices near my home.
You really have to wonder if that family name gave him a subtle push into his choice of profession.
It's curious that he's an orthopedic surgeon.

As mentioned in the intro to this chapter, not all name/occupation coincidences are directly related. Some have more of a humorous irony relativity.

For example.
George Pennypacker with his choice of work is right on the money for this sort of correlation.
He's a banker!

Then there's **Dr. Paul Looney**.
Maybe it was a full moon when he chose his livelihood.
He's a psychiatrist!

·~·

Is this for real?

Dr. Lester Plack,who no doubt is known as Les Plack, maybe felt a subliminal stirring from his name for his life's work.

Yep, he's a dentist!

·~·

Just a mere coincidence?

Dr. Timothy Bowser, DVM

If your dog had a fall, you know who to call.

·~·

Here's a man who answered a calling from above, and maybe felt a tweak from his name too.

Enjoyed your sermon ...

Rev. Paul Divine

·~·

If the family name is Burns, sooner or later someone in the clan had to get into firefighting for a career.

And that's what **Larry Burns** did.

He indeed is a fireman.

·~·

Now I know appellative determinism is more than just a theory.

There are a lot of real estate agents out there.

One of them has the name ...

Bob Housefinder

This find tickles me for some reason.

Here's a chap who saw the forest thru the trees, and became a professor of forestry ...

William Bramble

Ever walk among the bramble in the woods?

This find could only be better if the surgeon's name were Scalpel. But it's a slice anyway.

Dr. James Carver, you're wanted in surgery.

He's a surgeon!

Wouldn't it be something if I had a plumber with the last name Plumber?

If I did, that would just about unplug any doubts about the validity of my theory.

But how about **Edward Plummer** who indeed is a plumber!

There's a joke that goes, "we're called patients because the doctor is never on time for our appointment."

With that in mind, would you choose **Dr. Eugene Tardy** for your physician?

No appellative determinism there, but I thought you'd like it. On second thought, maybe there is.

This fellow could be my foot doctor any time.

Dr Allen Korn, podiatrist

Don't you wonder if Dr. Korn said to himself back when, "I know I'm going into medicine for a profession, but what area should I specialize in? I got it, with my name podiatry should be a winner!"

⁓

Heart trouble?

Lots of cardiologists in the yellow pages to choose from. Maybe you'd think twice about calling ...

Dr. Robert Croke, heart specialist

He's got to get a lot of teasing throughout the years.

⁓

Some years ago I was visiting a friend who lives in a small town about a hundred miles from my home. I mentioned my name mania; it almost always produces an addition to my family of names.

He said, "heck, there's a doctor in town with the name of Sickley."

I scrambled for the phone book, and there it was...

Jerome Sickley M.D.

This appellative determinism stuff gets eerie at times.

⁓

If you were charged with murder, and needed a good defense, would you choose this barrister?

Bruce Deadman, attorney at law

A tale of two Rolands.

Dr. Roland Brush, dentist

Dr. Roland Wink, optometrist

This gets zany, doesn't it?

If you're in need of marriage counseling, you could do no better than …

Patricia Love, marriage counselor

Pat Love will get you back into marital bliss.

It must be a hoot to see this practitioner's name in the phone book or on the marquee above his place of business.

Dr. Lee Popwell, chiropractor

My theory subtly at work there.

Let's end this chapter with three more doctors.

I'm going to take poetic license on the first one. Instead of using the first name, I'll use the first name initial. I'm sure this health-care pro is well aware of the smiles and laughs the combination creates.

His first name is Paul, but using the initial …

Dr. P. Good, urologist

Then there's **Dr. Gordon Mitts**.

Guess what his specialty is.

No surprise, the hands. Just a wee bit of determinism there?

And lastly …

> **Dr. Royal Payne**, proctologist

Now that's humorous irony!

But maybe my appellative determinism theory is a bucket full of holes.

Let's have a look at the next chapter.

A name is a kind of face whereby one is known.

Thomas Fuller
1608-1661

12

Appellative Determinism Debunked

No doubt the name/occupation relativities in the preceding chapter are just a few that are out there. I wish
I had them all. If I did, I could firm-up my appellative
determinism theory all the more.

But maybe I'm wrong. I've come across many
names that beg to be associated with a certain livelihood, but aren't. Not all people with this sort of name
are impelled to the profession that his or her name
suggests.

The appellations I'm going to share with you in this
chapter debunk the determinism hypothesis. Many
owners of a certain occupation-suggestive name just
plain missed their calling.

For instance …

There's a **Dr. Robert Butt** who has a practice in a nearby town. Is he a proctologist?

No, he's a chiropractor.

Darn!

·~·

And then there's a fellow with the name **Ernest Hearing**.

Shouldn't he be an audiologist?

He's not even a doctor.

I can only dream.

·~·

How about **Lyon Trainer**.

Cutesy moniker given to him by his parents, but is he working with a circus doing what his name suggests?

Nope, he's a school teacher.

·~·

Some years ago a Mr. and Mrs. Shoes brought a son into the world. They gave him the stalwart name James.

Did **Jim Shoes** eventually become a physical education teacher?

'fraid not. No determinism there.

·~·

Another cutesy name is **Raynor Sheine**.

But did he grow up to be come a weatherman?

No such luck. Another calling missed.

There's a writer named **Beano Cook**.

Wouldn't it be a hoot if he owned and operated a beanery?

Debunked again.

You've seen those portable outhouses at construction sites and festival sites. I imagine it's quite a lucrative business.

I sure wish **John Pottie** were the founder and CEO of one of them.

But he isn't, and my theory is getting less convincing here.

Kerry Wood is a major league pitcher for the Chicago Cubs as of this writing.

If appellative determinism really worked, he'd be in the lumber cartage business.

Oh well, he does try to make hitters carry wood back to the dugout.

Speaking of carrying.

A member of our fair sex who works in an insurance office carries the unusual name **Carri Coffee**.

What a marvelous name for a worker in a Starbucks. Or even better, the owner.

Foiled again.

⋅⤳⋅

Here's a fairly well-known name, but again not doing the work that it impels.

Ernest Tidyman (now deceased) was a writer, but if determinism meant anything, his name would have nudged him into owning a custodial service.

⋅⤳⋅

The debunking continues.

Forrest Sawyer has a career in television.

Even though his first name has two r's in it, with that name he should be falling trees for a living.

Nomen est omen didn't mean a thing there.

⋅⤳⋅

Robin Crane should be president of *The Audubon Society*.

He (or she) probably isn't even a bird watcher.

⋅⤳⋅

Marlin Fitzwater is a former White House Press Secretary, but his name should've nudged him into being a deep-sea fisherman.

Marlin, you took the wind out of my sails.

⋅⤳⋅

Why isn't **Miles Span** CEO of a road construction company?

⋅⤳⋅

The name **Lionel Tiger** is probably more of parents being clever, but it didn't push him into a career in zoology as it should have.

⋅⌒⋅

Frank Grill is a name that makes its owner a red hot candidate for helping the determinism theory along by operating a hot dog stand.

Oh well …

⋅⌒⋅

I sure wish the authentic name **Penny Wise** were in the preceding chapter with its owner as a financial counselor.

Debunked again.

⋅⌒⋅

Clay Potter …

Why isn't he a potter?

⋅⌒⋅

And let's wrap this debunking up with a couple of ladies named Fannie.

First, there's **Fannie Feather**.

It's an authentic name, and if name determinism meant anything, she'd be a strip-tease dancer.

She isn't.

⋅⌒⋅

And then there's …

Fannie Hooker

She's just a housewife.

My appellative determinism theory is all done in fun, of course. Names and related occupations are just some of the coincidences of life.

But I leave this theme with a question:

Don't just a couple of the finds in Chapter 11 make you wonder?

Call me anything,
just don't call me collect!

origin unknown

13

The One and Only?

Have you ever wondered if you're the exclusive owner of your name?

The Social Security Administration tells us that there's about a half-million one-of-a-kind names in the United States. One person, and one person only, has that name.

Of course, if your name is Richard Johnson or Susan Smith, no doubt you share your name with many people. But the more uncommon your name, the more you might wonder about its singularity.

Every now and then the thought occurred to me that I might be the sole owner of my name; at least in America, and who knows, maybe the world. My surname isn't very common and my given name is rarely used in naming male babies. It's surprising how seldom I see or hear of another Bruce. During my thirty-four years as a family insurance agent, I didn't have more than two or three customers who share my first name.

So, not long ago, in this hi-tech age, I Googled my name. There's a certain college professor with my name, a scientist, and a few other persons of note who have my first and last name.

So much for my name being the one and only!

Some names, though, are so extraordinarily unique that the owners most likely are the sole possessors of that assigned appellation in the nation, and probably the world. I could check with the Social Security people, but I doubt if they'd co-operate.

As a dedicated name watcher, I've encountered many names that sure seem like there could be no other like it. Unless the owners of these names have a living relative with the same surname and given name, they have to be the only person in the world having to bear the looks, smiles, and comments that their unique moniker certainly would generate.

Some of the names I'm going to share with you are female names, so I can't be sure if the surname is original or the result of marriage. Nevertheless, the lady still has to carry on through life with her singular calling.

In Chapters three and four I showed you some zany

names that are probably one-of-a-kind, but they're the obvious product of the temporary insanity of some parents, you might say.

The names in this chapter are of a different sort. They're simply most unusual, and could very well be part of that one-of-kind category cited by the Social Security Administration.

So, let's have a look.

Is this fellow the proverbial wimpy guy who has sand kicked in his face at the beach, or is he a body builder to compensate for the appellation he has to carry around?

Meet ...

Melvin Wimp

I don't know if this lady's family name is the result of marriage, but that name and her given name combine for this special place in my book.

May I introduce ...

Fairybell Sapp

I attended college with this gal.

You've heard of the defense substance called Mace. If it's sprayed on you, it's no delight.

Meet my former classmate ...

Delight Mace

In my opening chapter I mentioned that many centuries ago people sometimes selected an item around the house for a second name.

Some of these names still exist today.

Say hello to ...

Orphia Outhouse

If you're a name collector, let it be known whenever you can. A "keeper" almost always comes your way.

My son's father-in-law, a former teacher, told me the name of the father of one of his students. It's a keeper.

I'd like you to meet ...

Bougle Dingus

Your author is the oldest of four children. When my two brothers and sister were babies, I remember my mother calling a pacifier a "pippy."

When this fellow's name came my way, I was reminded of the word.

Meet the possible one-and-only ...

Huxtable Pippey

I imagine this gent's name is of Germanic origin, and would be rather ordinary in Deutschland. But on this side of the pond I'm sure it draws a second look now and then.

May I present ...

Kermit Slobb

One definition of the word slob is a "sloppy or course person."

That definition is a good lead-in for our next name, which could very well be one-of-a-kind.

If this surname were mine, I think I'd pop for a few bucks and have it altered a bit.

Meet ...

Merrill Sloppy

Does the owner of this name grapple with a weight problem? Is she the opposite of what her name suggests? Is she the one-and-only?

Quite possible.

A big hug for ...

Sophronia Plump

This fellow would certainly qualify for the *My Name is a Poem* club.

No doubt his parents were going for the rhyme thing, and you have to wonder about the origin of the family name.

It definitely belongs in this chapter.

Hello to …

Tucker Fudpucker

How would you like to have the first name Bland?

If could be that in itself is a one-and-only, but when combined with this rather unusual surname, I think we have good case for singularity.

I'd like you to meet …

Bland Button

Think this name is one-of-a-kind?

It's about as unique as you can get, and I imagine that it belongs to one of our fair ladies.

May I introduce …

Crescent Dragonwagon

The surname here is probably Irish. Many Irish family names end in "oon", such as in Muldoon.

Combined with the selected given name, we have an excellent case for no other owner.

Presenting …

Whipple Filoon

This name tickles me for some reason, and I'm guessing that it belongs to no other.

Say good morning to …

Birch Pancake

This unique name is a good one to place right after Mr. Pancake's.

Now how many people could have this name …

Maple Hinkle

As mentioned in the introduction to this book, people's names fascinate me. I know my stash is just a small representation of the more entertaining half-million one-of-a-kind names that the Social Security Administration has on record.

I wish I had the lot of them.

Without comment , here are some more that I would like to believe stand alone on God's green earth.

My friends and now yours …

Carpus Yip

Egbert Rot

Digby Tickle

Tyndle Fooks

Burma Gooch

Delzita Whack

Esmond Fatter

Hooker Pepper

Narsisia Goosby

Belverd Needles

Tilghman Billions

Lavender Sidebottom

Tressanela Noosepickle

and

Providence Clutterbuck

And to think those just scratch the surface!

Everybody has a name; anybody has a name,
and everybody anybody does what he does
with his name, feels what he feels about his name,
likes or dislikes what he has to have with having
his name; in short, it is his name unless
he changes his name; unless he does what he likes
what he likes with his name.

Gertrude Stein
1874-1946

14

Change Your Name to What??

Do you like your name?

I'm satisfied with mine. Oh, a while back the name Bruce was used by the comedy world to give a name to a fellow who was "light in the loafers", but it never bothered me. I'm OK with the handle hung on me by my parents, and my family name is what it is (a short "u" by the way).

According to the occult science, numerology (founded by the Greek mathematician Pythagoras), the letters of your full name, along with your birth date, relate to numbers that, in combination, supposedly tell much about you and your destiny.

There's another system of belief called nameology. According to this science, the arrangement and length of your name may be holding you back from the success you deserve in life.

For quite awhile now I've been using the services of a certain chiropractor who had a rather lengthy surname. A decade or so into his career he heard about nameology, and consulted a nameologist. He was advised to shorten and somewhat rearrange his last name, and to change his middle name, which he did.

What can I say; his practice rarely gives him a free moment ever since.

I imagine that a person's name can have a subtle influence in the job market. If a Robert Adams and another fellow with one of the bizarre names in this book were vying for a position, all other factors being equal, I'd predict the Adams name would be the hiree.

But names can be deceiving. Many years ago in my college days during a summer vacation a friend of mine asked me if I'd be the escort of the daughter of a friend of his mother's who was visiting from another state.

I accepted, and at the appointed evening I was introduced to Wilma Schlief.

A name certainly not of the Sue Johnson genre, but Wilma was both a looker and a charmer, which amounted to a delightful evening. What's in a name.

So it goes with names. The moniker pinned on you

may or may not be to your liking, and depending on what you believe, may or may not be conducive to you being the best that you can be.

Every year about 100,000 Americans petition the courts to have their name changed. No doubt genuine dissatisfaction with one's given name and/or surname is the primary reason. Business appeal is another reason for initiating a change of name. It's quite common in the entertainment industry.

But some requests for a new name are just plain silly. Even so, many of them are approved.

Take the case of Michael Dengler.

He petitioned the court to change his legal name to a number. The number desired: 1069

Michael claimed the number "symbolizes my interrelationship with society, and conceptually reflects my personal and philosophical identity."

His petition was denied.

Upon appeal, the supreme court upheld the decision, but advised Dengler that the change could be done in letters.

Thus, either **Ten Sixty Nine** or **One Zero Six Nine** would be acceptable.

Amazing.

Then there's Earl Bottomlee.

He petitioned the court to have his name changed to **Aerlygodlet Wileyelectronspirit Leegravity**.

Why he wanted that zany name, I don't know, but his request was denied. The judge said that the name was absurd, and it would only be a handicap to Mr. Bottomlee.

How about this case.

Claiming that his name is too difficult to pronounce, one **Dinker Fatterpaker** petitioned the court to change it to **Deenker Flatterpaker**.

Boy, I tell ya.

The request was approved.

Evidently, sometimes a hobby or passion in life can be so important to a person that he or she is compelled to petition the court to have their name changed to reflect the intense interest.

Such as in the case of Henry Schiff.

His passion in life is having lizards as pets. He approached the court to have is name legally changed to **Henry Lizardlover**.

His request was granted, and our congrats, Henry.

⁓

A similar case is that of Peter Eastman.

His great passion in life is fishing, particularly for Trout.

It's a love so great that he petitioned the court to have his name changed to **Trout Fishing**.

The court took the bait and our compliments to you, Pete, or rather Trout, for your great catch!

⁓

Then there's Stefan Albert.

He never liked his given name, and didn't seriously consider changing it until he became fascinated with loons.

Stefan says, "I really like loons. Every summer I swim out on the lake, and try to join a flock of them."

People started calling him "loon", and he liked the sound of it. So he petitioned the court, and believe it or not, managed to legally change his name to **Truly Remarkable Loon**!

Looney.

⁓

Next case.

Now comes Jim McLellen.

He had a passion for listening to records played by the music machine we know as a jukebox.

His passion was so great that he asked the court to have his name changed to **Jukebox Jim**.

His request was granted.

I sure hope it's a life long passion for Jim ... er, Jukebox because it would be a silly name to have if he lost interest in playing records in a contraption with blinking lights around it.

I suppose he could go back to court.

⁘

Our next request of a name change story isn't based on a hobby or intense interest. It involves a fellow named Fred Koch, as in coke.

Fred grew weary of people mispronouncing his name, such as "kotch" or "cook", so he petitioned the court requesting his name be changed to **Frederick Coke-is it**.

His request was approved, but there's a little more to the story.

The Coca-Cola Company somehow got wind of this, and gave some legal resistance, claiming the slogan was a trademark. It was settle amicably, and Fred could keep his new name.

⁘

Now comes Michael Ascot.

Not a bad name to have, but he petitioned the court to have his name changed to **Michael John Silly Arse**.

Here's his reason:

He claimed the name change would be for the benefit of the starving Ethiopians. Michael said, "it must be humiliating to have to beg for food, so I thought I would do something very humiliating to help. This is the most humiliating thing I can think of."

I take it his effort was successful and the food-deprived Ethiopians are indeed grateful, Mike.

.⌒.

Sooner or later someone had to do it.

One Roy Schultz of North Pole, New York had his name legally change to **Santa C. Claus**.

Some of these name changes just sleigh me.

.⌒.

Next up, Rex Frink.

I could live with that name, but an idea for a name change came to him in a dream. Then he thought about it for nearly three years before petitioning the court.

The name requested: **Welcome Pleasure Freely**.

Rex says, "it's poetic; it speaks to me; it's a living name; I am the name; I'll always cherish it."

Based on that quote I guess his request was granted.

A Christian name it's not.

Speaking of Christian names, let's wrap-up this chapter with the ultimate name change.

A fellow named Bruce Strong, a college professor, decided that wasn't enough, and wanted to be God.

He petitioned a few courts in the United States to have his name changed to these rather lofty three letters, but his requests were denied.

He was so determined that he went before a judge on the island of Guam, and somehow had his name actually changed to **God**!

Pray tell, now what, Professor Strong?

Of the many requests for a change of name each year in our great country, it would be interesting to learn what percent are as zany as those I've just shared with you. Evidently, for some people, the name they carry is of all-consuming importance, or must reflect their life's passion.

To most of us, our name is just an assemblage of letters that we rent for a short time, and then it's sayonara.

If you know of an entertaining name-change story, please send it to me.

With a name like yours,
you might be any shape, almost.

Lewis Carroll
1832-1898

15

Potpourri

This chapter so-named because it's just a potpourri of anecdotes, observations, and questions involving names.

You've turned the pages up to here, so I imagine you're enjoying my effort to bring you some fun.

Let's have some more fun.

I have a great story that could've been stuffed in the occupation/name relativity chapter, but I saved it for here because it's a bit different.

If you decided to put on the feed bag at a Wendy's Hamburger outlet, and a young lady showing the name tag "Wendy" took your order, and you being in a playful mood said, "I suppose your last name is Hamburger", and she responded with, "as a matter of fact, it is", you'd be incredulous.

In the early 1960s before David Thomas founded the *Wendy's Hamburger* organization, a certain Mr. and Mrs. Hamburger brought a daughter into the world, and gave her the first name Wendy.

When Wendy was a highschooler she took a part-time job with the local Wendy's Hamburger outlet.

Wendy Hamburger could have indeed taken your order! I love it.

If two ladies named Mary Smith were out motoring, and collided on the road, you'd shrug and think of it as a so-so coincidence. After all, there are many Mary Smiths in the world.

In 1992, a **Kathleen Wolfenden** was behind the wheel of her car, and had the misfortune of colliding with another car driven by a fellow member of the fair sex.

The other driver's name? **Kathleen Wolfenden**!

The two women were no relation, and had never heard of one another.

Fascinating.

Here's a name coincidence tale of a different sort.

A fellow with the name **Kenneth Pigeon** was caught breaking into a commercial building.

A security guard nabbed Pigeon in the act. His name: **Reginald Peacock**.

Then Peacock called the police. The name of the arresting officer: **George Bird**.

A feather in their caps and not a peep from the perp.

Staying with the theme of arrests and names coincidences, at rare times the name on the police blotter will relate in some way to the charge.

Have a look at these …

A gent with the name **Heywood Tipsey** was arrested and taken to the station. The charge: drunk driving.

And then there's the case of **William Sober**. He also got the attention of the law while driving. He too was taken in. His offense: drunk driving (what else?).

How about **Joy Love**. That's her real name, and she was hauled by the ear to the police station. The charge, of course, was prostitution.

And finally, there's **Joseph Bustinski**.

He too got on the arrest records. With his name the charge could only be breaking and entering.

It was.

No doubt the four preceding arrest/name anecdotes are just a few that have found their way to the arrest logs of the law.

I wish I had them all.

Ever hear of a palindrome?

It's a word, phrase, or sentence that reads the same forward and backward. The word toot is a palindrome.

A name palindrome is rare, but I've found a couple of them during my constant vigil.

Surely the parents of the two fellows with the names to follow knew they were creating a palindrome when naming the baby. I wonder what came first, the desire for the first name or the fun of pinning a palindrome on the newcomer.

Meet ...

Mark Kram

and

Robert Trebor

Maybe you know of a person with a palindrome name. I'd sure like to have it.

Is your name hard to spell?

Can you imagine little **Chester Grzeszcyczyn** learning to spell his name?

Chances are, as an adult, he still has to pause every now and then to remember the correct sequence of the letters. I wonder if his friends call him "eyechart."

It would be interesting to know what per cent of

male names are juniors. That is, having been given the same name as their father.

How many can say they're a junior with the family name Senior?

Say hello to ...

Vincent Senior Jr.

How many people can say they have the same letters in their first name as in their last name, excluding names in which the first and last name are the same?

Very few I'm sure.

I'd like you to meet ...

Amy May

and

Gary Gray

I don't know if this gal's name combo is a result of marriage, but if it isn't, her parents were sure in an alliterative mode when her name was assigned.

May I introduce ...

Penelope Penopolis

Here are a couple of cases of morbid irony.

I have no idea how many tall-building window washers have fallen to their death in the last hundred years or so, but I would guess very few.

Some years ago a fellow named **Will Drop**, a window washer by occupation, did indeed come loose from his moorings, and drop to his demise.

Similarly, how many people have lost their lives from a bee sting? It's rare. A lady with the name **Michelle Honey** incurred a bee sting, and the toxic effect caused her death.

What are the odds?

How many of us can say that our first, middle, and last names are the same?

This is something else.

A Mr. and Mrs. Dominick evidently thought they'd honor their family name with all three names of their new baby boy. Either that, or they couldn't think of any other names for his first and middle name.

Meet …

Dominick Dominick Dominick

I think he should get a special discount at Dominick's

Sometimes in this name collecting business you hit on a name that seems to beg a question or two.

Here's what I mean …

John Daddio

What's he like? Is he a hipster? Wassup John?

Philander Knox

Is he a Lothario? If married, does he stray?

Audrey Jew

What's her religion? Does she have a religion?

Patricia Cake

Is she known to her friends as Patty Cake?

Jack Ripper

If single, does he get dates? Do the ladies stay afar?

Douglas Smellie

Does he offend? What was life like in grade school?

Curt Jester

Funny guy? Was he the class clown?

Gertrude Messmaker

The opposite of her name or is she a slob?

Ronald Wierdo (correct spelling)

Easy to know? A bit weird?

Angela Angel

Is she angelic? Hard to get along with?

⁓

And lastly, if you asked me what's the most bizarre name I've ever found, I'd have an answer.

Imagine a surname the same as an infectious disease, and the given name the same as a well-known brand of a petroleum jelly.

I'd like you to meet…

Vaseline Malaria

A truly bizarre name.

One more chapter to go.

Get ready.

"A very good name, indeed", said Mr. Pickwick,
wholly unable to suppress a smile.

The Pickwick Papers
Charles Dickens
1812-1870

16

On the Naughty Side

I have to begin this chapter by saying that if suggestive humor makes you uncomfortable, I recommend you not read the remainder of the book.

Some years ago when it crossed my mind that I might some day write a humorous book using my bag of names, it never occurred to me that a chapter with this theme would be included.

As time pressed on, it became apparent to me that there are quite a number of names out there that are ribaldly suggestive in the idiom of our times. And it's fascinating that the owners of such a name dutifully live with it, and face society with their heads held high.

I don't end my book with this theme because a bit of titillation sells, or because of adolescent carry-over (still there, though), but because the names exist and I want to share them with you.

So, putting our moral indignation aside, let's have a go at it. By the way, a humorous definition of moral indignation is "jealousy with a halo."

During the last hundred years or so, certain words in our culture have been stolen and corrupted to create another meaning. The word "gay" is a good example. There was a time when a gay person was thought to be joyous and lively. No longer does that definition apply.

This has happened to a certain extent in the realm of people's names.

For example, most fellows with the given name Richard assume the nickname of either Dick, Rich, or Rick. Unfortunately, sometime along the way, the Dick option was seized and sullied to be used as a vulgarism for the male member.

This nickname, which is vastly common, doesn't have a suggestive impact, of course, unless it's adjoined with a suitable surname.

The first time I came across a suggestive first and last name combination in which the owner with the given name Richard who goes by the nickname Dick was way back in the late 1950s when I was a Private in Uncle Sam's army. This was long before I became infected with onomatomania.

A likeable chap in the same company to which I was assigned was born Richard Stiff. He (or his parents) chose to informally use the Dick option, and thus became known by the startling handle of **Dick Stiff**!

Surprisingly, to my knowledge, none of his fellow soldiers, including me, teased him or even commented on it behind his back. The obvious remained unsaid, and I sometimes wondered why he went with that particular Richard modifier in relation to his family name.

Fast forward twenty years or so when I started to jot-down unusual names. Since then, I've discovered quite a number of surnames that have the given name Richard, and if the owner's selected nickname is Dick, combine to make one heckuva salty moniker.

In the names to follow, with the exception of Mr. Short and Mr. Rising, whom I know use the D-name, I'm uncertain what Richard alternative the owner has chosen, if any. I imagine most of them go by the same option as Mr. Stiff.

Meet ...

Dick Fell
Dick Fitts
Dick Hard
Dick Head
Dick Short

Dick Wood
Dick Bangs
Dick Rising
Dick Wiener
Dick Trickle
Dick Seeman
Dick Mountjoy
Dick Schwantz
and
Dick Passwater

The D-name can also be a surname. It's not very common, but you see it every now and then.

A large corporation has the name A.B. Dick, no doubt the initials and surname of its founder. Then there's television comedy actor named Andy Dick. Television and motion picture actor Tim Allen was born Timothy Allen Dick.

Nothing suggestive in the above names, but when certain given names are joined in combination with the surname, entries for this chapter can occur.

I'd like you to meet …

Ima Dick
Harry Dick
and
Mylene Dick

There's another male name that has snuck its way into the modern idiom, and been degraded in reference to the male appendage.

That being Peter.

I don't know when this fine biblical name was co-opted for that usage, but when the name match-ups to follow were given to the little newcomer, either the parents didn't know or didn't care. Perhaps in a few cases the naming took place before this particular appellation slipped into slang.

I'd like to introduce …

Peter Dick
Peter Rash
Peter Zipper
Peter Harder
Peter LaCock
and
Peter Dangles

⸎

Used in a surname, Peter usually appears as Peters or Peterson, but not always.

Say hello to …

Seymour Peter

⸎

Certain words have been borrowed and degraded into anatomical vulgar usage for the ladies too. Specifically, I'm referring to pussy, beaver, and bush.

I have a fun story involving the first word in that trio. The name surely had to have been selected by the parents before the bawdy connotation came into being.

In the early 1900s a Mr. and Mrs. Palmgren were honored with the birth of a daughter. For reasons only known to them, they were impelled to name her Pussy.

I don't know how long **Pussy Palmgren** lived, but it could very well be that she was with us long enough to have to endure the smiles and chuckles of polite society.

As for the other two words in that trio of borrowed words, I'd like you to meet …

Harry Bush

and

Harry Beaver

Staying with those two surnames, I discovered the names of a married couple whose family name match-up is nothing less than hilarious.

Imagine their engagement announcement in the local newspaper. It probably appeared something like this:

Kathleen Beaver and **Frank Bush** announce their

betrothal. The wedding is planned for next June, etc., etc..

.⌣.

How about the surnames involved in this wedded couple.

Imagine the bride choosing to keep both family names hyphenated. The wedding invitation had to be a hoot.

None other than **Janet Beaver** and **Gary Trimmer** entered holy matrimony.

Janet Beaver-Trimmer?

.⌣.

Here are a couple of name/profession relativities that further suggest the validity of "appellation determinism", the theme of Chapter 11.

It's best that I saved them for here.

Presenting ...

> **Dr. Peter Painless**, gynecologist
> **Dr. Alan Cockburn**, urologist

.⌣.

Sometimes foreign names, which wouldn't raise an eyebrow in their native country, can be quite a howl when heard by we of the English language.

Considering the billion-plus people in the Far East, I imagine oriental names could provide almost endless examples of names of this sort.

I have five of them for you.

A hearty welcome to …

Fu King

Fook Yu

Well Hung

Hung Long

and

Ho Lee Fook

Here's an oriental surname with an English given name.

Meet …

Harry Dong

The German language can also produce some hilarious names when seen and heard from the English perspective.

Gutentag to …

Karl Fucker

Arnold Fardt

Hans Dumfart

and

Anke Fuckerman

Then we have a couple of German surnames with English given names.

Say hello to …

John Schitt

and
Timothy Schitter

I came across a name no doubt of mid-Eastern origin that should generate a smile now and then on this side of the pond.

Introducing …

Ashit Kikani

Occasionally we all see a name in print that gives us pause for its pronunciation. I have a friend whose surname is spelled Orlikiewicz, which is certainly a puzzler. It's pronounced orluh skev'itch.

I have a few names, not so complicated in spelling, but how are they pronounced? Seriously, I don't know because I found them in print.

Any help?

May I present …

Erin Urine

Marcu Fux

Linda Kuntz

Robert Aass

Michael Asso

William Boner

Carolyn DePenis

and

Elizabeth Izabichie

I have three more marriage-made-in-heaven match-ups for you.

The wedding announcement for this one must've been a hoot from the printers to the recipients.

One **Carrie Ann Cockman** accepted the marriage proposal of none other than **Donald Dickman**.

The **Cockman/Dickman** nuptials. Wow!

Then there's **Armenia Funk** (possibly the one and only?)

Cupid's arrow sent her to **Howard Goff**. They married. Dare she keep both names?

Armenia Funk-Goff

And we have **Mary Hooker**.She married no other than **Elmer Tramp**.

Mary Hooker-Tramp?

This one is just from my imagination.

There's actually a fellow with the name **Andre Tits**.

Wouldn't it be something else if **Geneva Nipple** became his bride?

I can only dream.

I have a question …

Do **Penny Focks** and **Jack Orf** write their names very, very carefully?

Just wondering.

You haven't closed the book. You must be having fun. I know I am. Let's wrap it all up with my dear friends ...

Early Lay
Fonda Cox
David Kock
Helen Tiddy
Pat Hiscock
Oral Sexton
Jack Mehoff
Joyce Bangs
Phalia Tinkle
Harry Titlow
Phyllis Screws
French Tickner
Lillian Copsacker
and
Stephanie Snatchole

People's names can be fascinating, can't they?

I close with a quote from a philosopher of four centuries ago:

"Laughter is nothing else but sudden glory arising from some sudden conception of some eminency in ourselves, by comparison with infirmity of others, or with our own formerly."

Thomas Hobbes
1588-1679

I hope you've had a few moments of "sudden glory." *Ciao.*

About Your Author

I was born in Chicago, and lived there until age eight when my parents moved twenty-five miles west to suburban Downers Grove. This has been my home town ever since.

While raising a family, being an insurance agent kept them fed with a roof over their heads. Now retired, this is my first book. Did I mention golf?

E-mail: broos36@sbcglobal.net

References

Dunkling, L.A., *First Names First*, Universe Books, 1977

Hook, J. N., *Family Names*, MacMillan, 1982

Smith, E.C., *American Surnames*, Chilton Books, 1969

Stein, L., *Clues to Our Family Names*, Heritage Books, 1986

Wells, E., *What to Name the Baby*, Garden City, 1953

Magazines

Newspapers

Telephone books

School Year books

Anything (and anyone) with a "keeper"

www.ingramcontent.com/pod-product-compliance
Lightning Source LLC
Chambersburg PA
CBHW022253290526
45785CB00015B/765